Basics of E-Business

Roby Jose Ciju

CONTENTS

INTRODUCTION

With the advent of e-businesses and e-commercial transactions, the number of internet users who rely on internet for their buying and selling transactions has gone up considerably. E-Commerce is the buzz word in this modern technology-empowered era and there are numerous entrepreneurial opportunities awaiting creative entrepreneurs of all sorts in the field of e-commerce.

What is World Wide Web (WWW)?

The World Wide Web (WWW or W3) is a collection of websites which can be accessed via the Internet using a web browser such as Firefox, Google Chrome, Opera, and Internet Explorer. WWW is controlled by the World Wide Web Consortium (W3C), the international standards organization for the World Wide Web. Major objective of W3C is the development of standards for the World Wide Web.

What is a Website?

A website is a collection of web pages where the landing page is called 'homepage' and all other pages that can be accessed from home page are known as 'web pages'. After developing a website using relevant software applications (for example, 'Dreamweaver with PHP), it must be hosted on a web server, which is accessible via internet through a unique Internet address given to the website known as a 'Uniform Resource Locator' (URL). A beginner in the field of web development may log on to http://www.w3schools.com, a popular website that contains web development tutorials to gain some exposure on this topic.

What is Internet?

The Internet is a collection of all interconnected computer networks that are available worldwide. The internet functions are based on a set of standards called 'Internet Protocol' (IP) and each internet network is given an IP address. All internet networks that are globally available are interlinked by a broad spectrum of networking technologies. Three major networking technologies are,

1. Electronic Networking Technology
2. Wireless Networking Technology
3. Optical Networking Technology

A service provider that provides internet access to its customers so that they can connect to the internet using wire line or wireless or fibre-optic connections is called an Internet Service Provider (ISP).

CONCEPT OF E-BUSINESS

E-Business may be defined as any business activity that is carried out successfully with the wide application of information and communication technologies (ICT) with a major focus on information management and strategy. E-Marketing is a subset of E-Business and E-Commerce is a subset of an E-Marketing. An e-Business is also called a digital business or an online business or electronic business. First and foremost requirement for venturing into an online business is a well-designed website. Other important features required are E-commerce integration, integration of essential software applications, website registration, and website promotion.

Creating a Website for Your E-Business

It is easy. You can do it yourself or employ a professional web designer. If you plan to do it yourself, what you need is to download an appropriate website template from the internet. There are a number of website templates available on the internet for free download. Make sure that you have necessary software applications that are required for a website creation such as content management software, Dream Weaver, Wamp Server, Core FTP, Adobe Image Ready, Photoshop and similar software applications. Most of these software applications are available for free download from the internet. When it comes to the designing part of the website, you may rely on web designing tutorials available with W3Schools or any other free online tutorials to learn the basics.

If you find that designing your website all by yourself is a tedious task, then you may employ reputed professional web designing firms of your choice. Even if this is the case, website content and structure must be finalized by your managerial team, which should be based on your e-business strategy. Nothing can replace basic business planning and you must have a clear idea about how your website should look like; what information it should present to your customers; how your customers should interact with your website and how your products and services should be presented on the website. In fact, a well-designed website is the starting point toward a successful E-business venture.

Integration of E-Commerce Applications

Integration of E-commerce applications is an inevitable part of the e-business website so that clients can go through the listing of products and services; place the order using online shopping cart facility and do the payment using payment processing facility. Payment gateway services are provided by many private and public sector banks and other market players. Integrated cross-functional software applications are now becoming affordable even for small businesses. Most of these software applications integrate a number of functions such as, CRM (customer relationship management); ERP (enterprise resource planning); SCM (supply chain management and selling chain management); E-Procurement; Enterprise Application Integration; Business Intelligence, Knowledge Management, and Decision Support Systems.

Web Strategies: Key Features Required for Homepage

If you are creating a website for your E-Business, then homepage of your website MUST have the following features.

1. Technical Information about Products and Services
2. Technical Information about Prices
3. Background Information about the Firm (e.g.: 'about us' or 'company history' web pages)
4. Information about Where the Products/Services are sold (e.g.: 'client testimonials' web page)
5. Links to Other Information Sources (e.g.: 'Useful Links' web page)
6. Links to Trade Associations (e.g.: 'Web Directory' or 'Trade Directory' web pages)
7. Online Ordering Facility
8. Online Payment Facility
9. Online Communities or Discussion Forums
10. Customized and Unique Content
11. Password Protection
12. Assured Confidentiality and User Privacy

WEBSITE: KEY FEATURE OF AN E-BUSINESS

A well-designed website is a key feature of an e-business. While designing the website, keep the design simple and clean. Make it easy to navigate from page to page. Use relevant images on the website. Make it easy to contact you by providing a contact form. Another important point is to make the website visible on the internet by using search engine optimization techniques.

Major steps of starting an online business are, (i)finding a suitable domain name for your business and registering it, (ii) building a website, (iii) hosting the website with an affordable and reliable company, and (iv) get people to visit your website and increasing website traffic.

Domain Registration

Website registration is done in two sessions: Domain registration and registration for hosting services. 'Domain Name' is the name of your website and that name must be registered with a domain registrar. GoDaddy is currently world's No.1 domain registrar and the website can be reached at www.godaddy.com. There are other domain registrars as well, such as 'HostGator' and 'NameCheap'.

Website Hosting

Once a website is created and registered with a domain registrar, now it's time to launch the website on the internet. Most of the domain registrars also provide website hosting services.ther eare

Other Important Features

SSL (Security Socket Layer) certificates, search engine visibility and such other additional features are also available with them for an extra cost. SSL feature makes sure that your website is secure enough for the clients to enter sensitive data on the website. SSL is an essential feature for an e-business website. Search engine visibility feature ensures that your website is visible across all the search engines such as google, bing, and yahoo.

MODELLING AN E-BUSINESS

Fundamental step that goes into the development of your E-business model is a well-thought out e-business plan.

Figure 1 illustrates the steps involved in the preparation of a final business plan.

Figure 1: Preparation of a Business Plan

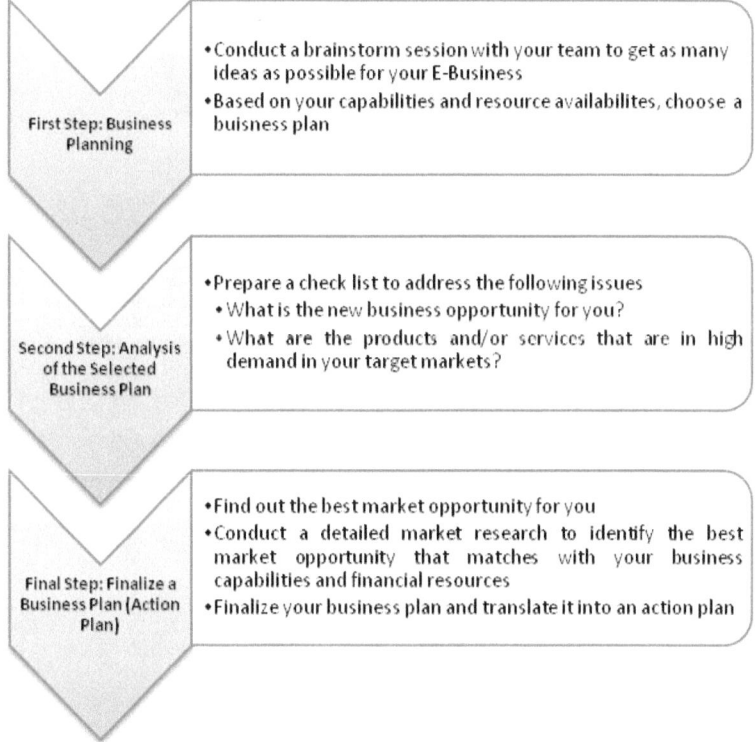

The action plan is ready for the establishment of your e-business and you have identified current market opportunities that suit your business plan. You have a managerial team in place to assist you with your venture and you have a panel of expert consultants or 'Subject Matter Experts' to provide you with technical guidance. Now it's time to finalize a model for your E-Business. Figure 2 illustrates the steps involved in the preparation of a business model.

Figure 2: Preparation of E-Business Model

First Step: Finalize Technology Portfolio and Technology Vendors

- Choose the most essential software applcations
- What kind of digital/electronic/information technologies should be chosen for your business?
- Finalize the portfolio of digital technologies that are to be employed in your e-business
- Finalize technology vendors
- Choose reliable cost effective software applications
- Choose the best technology partners and vendors

Second Step: Finalize Core Competencies and Features Required

- Every business should be unique in its products and/or services and therefore while modelling a business, its core competencies and unique features must be decided carefully. Answer the following questions in order to conclude the best features that are to be included in your e-business model.
- What are the core competencies of your business?
- What are the assets to your E-business? Is it its well experienced staff or its large network of subject matter experts or its technological innovations and so on?
- How do you differ from your closest competitors?
- Based on the answers, you may chart out a core competency chart for your organization that highlights your organizations core competencies and unique features

Third Step: Finalize Business Model

- Is the operational cost of this E-Business Model within your capabilities?
- Is this business model best suited to take maximum advantage of the current market opportunities?

Final Step: Analyze Business Model

- What are strengths/weaknesses/opportunities/threats for your business model?
- Who are your target customers?
- How do you add value to customer experience?
- How do you make money?
- How do you finance your company?
- How do you get and retain your customers?
- How do you attract talented people to work for you?
- What software applications are best for your business?

Based on regular analysis, the current E-Business Model may be improved according to your business requirements as the implementation process goes on smoothly.

E-BUSINESS, MAJOR DRIVING FACTORS

Several factors play important roles in the fast expansion and advancement of e-businesses such as fast growth of internet market, affordable computing devices, reliable service providers and tech-savvy young generation. A detailed account of these factors is given below.

1. Fast growing internet market and net-savvy population
2. Speed and dynamics of the internet
3. Less capital investments as compared to traditional business models
4. Faster service to customers and enhanced customer loyalty
5. Flexibility in order fulfilment
6. Just in Time delivery of products and/or services
7. Accessibility to a global market
8. Virtual platform for marketing and distribution
9. Outsourcing opportunities
10. Transparency and visibility
11. Availability of affordable enterprise software applications
12. Availability of handheld and mobile computing devices
13. Wireless web applications and reliable service providers

Points to Remember in an E-Business

- ✓ Think Big; Start Small
- ✓ Build on Success
- ✓ Build, Launch and Learn
- ✓ Scale Fast

E-MARKETING

E-Marketing may be defined as a marketing activity that make use of electronic technologies such as the use of a computerized, networked environment and the Internet for the distribution, promotion and sales of products and/or services to the target segments. In a nutshell, E-marketing enables product sales and marketing over the Internet by making use of digital marketing tools. Synonyms of E-marketing are, internet marketing; digital marketing; electronic marketing and online marketing. Major objective of an e-marketing campaign is to bring more web traffic to a website so that a major percent of this web traffic is converted into potential customers.

Website Traffic

Web traffic is a term used to determine the number of visitors that visit a specific website and the number of pages they visit. Website traffic indicates how many people visit your website and how many web pages are viewed during a specific period of time. It is possible to monitor web traffic using specific technologies called 'Search Analytics'. One of the reputed websites that provide reliable data on web traffic is Alexa. Alexa traffic rank of your website is available at www.alexa.com.

Page Rank

'Page Rank', the name given after Larry Page, the founder of Google Inc, is an algorithm invented by Google team to determine the reputation of a website. High page rank of a website means that the website has a good reputation.

TRENDS IN E-MARKETING

Some of the current trends in E-marketing are referral marketing, social media marketing, search engine marketing, e-mail marketing, content or article marketing and web directory listing.

Referral Marketing

Referral marketing is a marketing strategy based on referrals where products and/or services are introduced to a new set of customers through referrals.

Social Media Marketing

Internet marketing that makes use of social media websites such as Twitter (www.twitter.com), YouTube (www.youtube.com), LinkedIn (www.linkedin.com), Google Plus (www.google.com/plus), and Facebook (www.facebook.com) for bringing more web traffic is termed as 'Social Media Marketing'. By using Twitter you may post 'tweets' about your products and services to a wide online audience while YouTube allows you to launch promotional videos of your products and services online. LinkedIn allows you to create a business page for your business and also allows you to have direct access to millions of professionals worldwide from your chosen field of profession. Currently Facebook is the leading social media site worldwide with billions of subscribers and having a Facebook account for your business is worth the effort on all accounts. Google Plus, comparatively a new entrant in the social media circle, is slowly garnering strength as a powerful social networking site.

E-Mail Marketing

Email marketing is a direct marketing strategy where a commercial message is popularised among a group of people, normally registered customers, using electronic mail. E-mail has now become a powerful communication media and is being commercially exploited as a cost-effective marketing tool by many digital firms. Mass e-mail sending campaigns has now become as common as newspaper ad inserts. Another area where e-mail power is being used is in sending mass newsletters to the customers. Sending personalised newsletter is also considered as an efficient customer contact program. Another important advantage of e-mail marketing is that a strong customer database can be built up through newsletters and mass e-mail sending campaigns over a period of time. This customer database serves as the strong foundation of your E-Business. So when you launch your E-business, please don't forget to send out weekly or monthly newsletters on a regular basis to the registered members so that they keep informed about latest developments with respect to your online business activities.

Search Engine Marketing (SEM)

The software application that is used for searching information over the internet is known as a 'Search Engine'. Top search engines in the world are Google (www.google.com), Yahoo (www.yahoo.com), Ask Jeeves (www.ask.com), and Bing (www.bing.com). The first and foremost principle of 'Search Engine Marketing' (SEM) that is to be applied while creating a website is to make it search engine friendly at the time of web designing itself. This can be done by choosing the right keywords (sometimes 'keywords' are referred as 'tags') for writing the website content. Providing an appropriate title for each web page based on the content displayed on that page also makes it search engine friendly.

Second principle of SEM that is applicable here is listing of the website with all popular search engines available over the internet. As a part of online marketing campaign, a website needs to be registered with all popular search engines. If the website is targeted by the local customers, then it needs to be registered with the local search engines also.

Third principle of SEM is 'Search Engine Optimization' (SEO). If you want your website's content to be appeared in search result pages of popular search engines, then your website must be optimized for search engine visibility. There are certain set of rules to be followed while creating/designing a website. For more information, 'Google Webmaster Tools' may be referred.

Search Engine Optimization (SEO)

Websites can increase their web traffic by registering their URLs on search engines and through search engine optimization (SEO). The most important objective of SEO is to bring more traffic to your website by increasing your website's visibility in search engines. Figure 3 illustrates 'SEO' process in detail. Since Google is the most visited search engine in the world, 'Google Search Engine' is taken as an example.

Figure 3: Search Engine Optimization Process

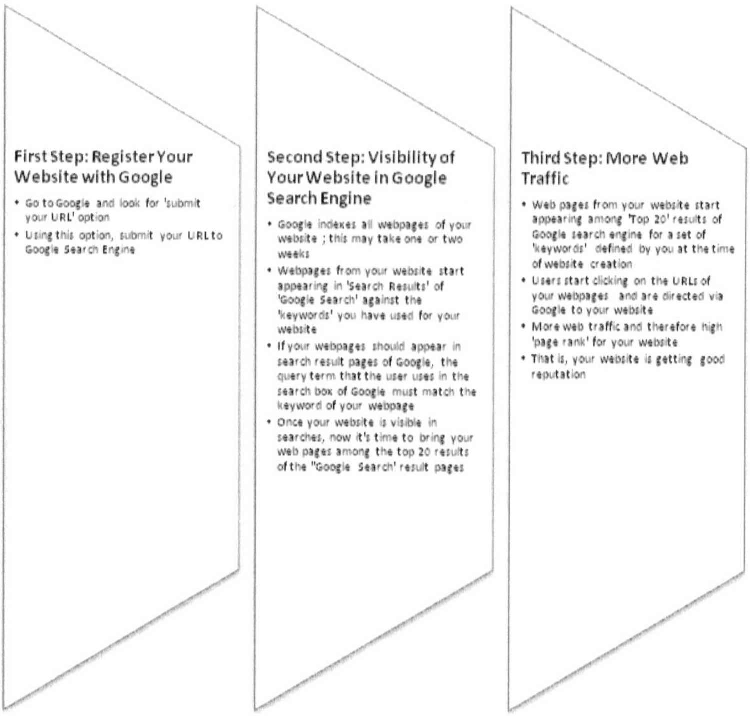

First Step: Register Your Website with Google
* Go to Google and look for 'submit your URL' option
* Using this option, submit your URL to Google Search Engine

Second Step: Visibility of Your Website in Google Search Engine
* Google indexes all webpages of your website ; this may take one or two weeks
* Webpages from your website start appearing in 'Search Results' of 'Google Search' against the 'keywords' you have used for your website
* If your webpages should appear in search result pages of Google, the query term that the user uses in the search box of Google must match the keyword of your webpage
* Once your website is visible in searches, now it's time to bring your web pages among the top 20 results of the "Google Search' result pages

Third Step: More Web Traffic
* Web pages from your website start appearing among 'Top 20' results of Google search engine for a set of 'keywords' defined by you at the time of website creation
* Users start clicking on the URLs of your webpages and are directed via Google to your website
* More web traffic and therefore high 'page rank' for your website
* That is, your website is getting good reputation

Heavy website traffic and higher Page Rank of a website are indicators of a well-reputed website. You may try 'Google Website Optimizer', a tool provided by Google to increase SEO of your website. Refer http://www.google.com/websiteoptimizer/tutorials.html for more information.

Search Analytics

'Search analytics' is a term used to refer the analysis of search engine data such as search volume trends, user profile, keyword monitoring, search history and so on. Search analytics is very useful in search engine marketing (SEM) and search engine optimization (SEO) as search analytics helps web masters improve website performance on search engines.

Web Analytics

Web analytics is a tool for measuring web traffic where the analysis of a website is done by collecting and analysing web data using third party cookies. Web analytics may be used as a business and market research tool. Analysing your website's performance time to time provides deep insights into your online business. There are several applications available online for website analysis. One such tool is Google Analytics from Google Inc. Please refer http://www.google.com/analytics for more information.

Marketing via Online Advertisements and Affiliate Programs

Online advertising strategies such as contextual advertising and advertising based on customer behaviour are the best and the most cost-effective ad choices for an E-business. There are a plethora of online advertisement options available on the internet. However, 'Google Adwords' program, an online advertisement program run by Google Inc., is one of the best in the industry.

Internet giants such as amazon.com, godaddy.com, google.com and many other reputed 'dot com' businesses offer 'affiliate marketing programs' for interested parties whereby affiliates are supposed to sell their products and/or services online. Almost all of them follow a commission-based revenue model where the affiliate business gets a per cent of the total transaction value as commission when a transaction is carried out through the affiliate business/website.

Content Marketing

Content marketing is a marketing strategy based on the creation and sharing of quality content with potential customers. Two types of content marketing are article marketing and blog marketing. Major objectives of content marketing are to generate leads, to increase sales by driving more web traffic to the target website, and to improve customer relations.

Article Marketing and Blog Marketing

Marketing your products and services online by writing high-quality articles and then publishing them with leading article directories is called article marketing. In blog marketing, marketers write blogs on related subjects and post them in popular blog directories. While choosing article or blog directories, remember to choose only those directories with a high Page Rank. Many free software applications are available online to check the page rank of a website.

Article/blog marketing is essential for bringing in much needed website traffic for the target website. You may employ some staff exclusively for writing blogs and articles for your online business.

Web Directory Listing

Listing your website with reputed web directories is another web strategy that webmasters all over the world are using to increase their web traffic as well as to build their website's reputation. There are a number of web directories available on the internet where listing may be done either for free or for a fee. You may choose either only free listing services or both free and paid listing services as per your business requirements. However make sure that you go for only the best web directories such as Dmoz (www.dmoz.org). Another web directory that is quite popular among e-marketers is Yahoo directory.

E-COMMERCE

E-commerce may be defined as the broad application of information and communication technologies to facilitate the movement of money, products and/or services, and information across target segments. E-commerce is nothing but the application of information technology in commercial activities. Actually it may be said that an e-business survives on its successful e-commerce applications. E-Commerce is a subset of both E-Business and E-Marketing as illustrated in Figure 4.

Figure 4: Definition of E-Commerce

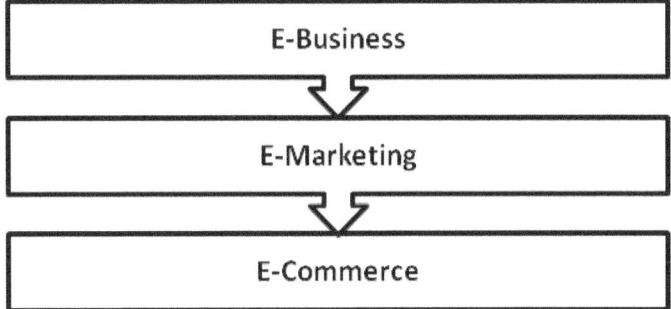

SCOPE OF E-BUSINESS

It is fairly easy to transform a traditional business into an E-Business. But what you need for this transition is a well-thought out business plan; a technology empowered work environment and an expert team of tech-savvy people. E-businesses are becoming easy to conduct in comparison with traditional business models; in the latter, parties interact in person compromising very much on their time and money while E-Business ventures are both time efficient and cost efficient.

Some of the best examples for profitable E-Business models are business consultancy services; digital publishing services; entrepreneurship development through e-education; e-retailing of food and agro-commodities; online distribution and marketing services for business firms, online tutoring services and online human resource recruitment services.

Business Consultancy Services

Considering the wide gap existing in the field of knowledge dissemination, it can be stated beyond doubt that consultancy is a field where IT and digital media can be successfully employed for making a huge impact on the lives of businesspersons and entrepreneurs.

E-Marketing Services

Electronic and digital media also helps producers/suppliers in forging direct relationships with potential buyers eliminating all middlemen in between and thus providing a transparent platform for healthy negotiation so that producers/suppliers can demand a fair price for their commodities and services.

Digital Publishing

Right information is the key to any successful business activity. Digital publications allow all interested parties to have direct access to right information instantly.

E-Retailing

E-retailing is another area where huge potential exists for a net-savvy entrepreneurs and business persons. More and more people are now depending on internet for their purchases and this trend is only going to increase considering the fast pace of the spread of internet awareness among the population.

E-BUSINESS MODELS

THREE standard e-Business models that are still popular among business strategists are, B2B, B2C and C2C.

Business-to-Business (B2B)

B2B model focuses on market link transaction between two businesses where an established network of suppliers and buyers is used for business transactions. For example, online B2B directories

Business-to-Consumer (B2C)

In B2C, a business tries to reach its target customers through an established digital system to sell its products and/or services. For example, online shopping sites

Consumer-to-Consumer (C2C)

In C2C model, focus is on consumer-to-consumer transactions and interactions.

Potential Business Models for a Technology-Empowered Environment

However, in this era of technological innovations, standard business models sometimes may not work due to the want of regular technological upgrades and highly skilled employees. In this scenario, two other business models may be considered for your E-Business: These are, 'the improvement-based business model' and 'the revenue-based business model'.

The Improvement-Based Business Model

Improvement-based business models neither bring immediate profits nor focus on the sales volumes. Rather its focus is to use the Internet to enhance the internal efficiency of the business; to increase the effectiveness of business promotion and marketing; and most importantly to make positive changes in customer's attitude. For that matter, two important reasons behind a firm's creation of an E-Business are cost-effectiveness and internal efficiency. Other important products of an E-Business are brand building, database building, expanded customer service, and product and/or service enhancement through online information and customer feedback.

The Revenue-Based Business Model

Major focus of a revenue-based model is to create a steady revenue stream so that the business venture sustains itself for a long term. Revenue-based business models are of two types: the provider-based revenue approach or the user-based revenue approach. A comparison of both of these business models is given in the following table.

Comparison of E-Business Models

The Provider-Based Revenue Approach

Revenues are coming from other companies who want to reach the firm's website users/user database at a premium fee. Examples are, content sponsorship and retail alliances.

The User-Based Revenue Approach

Revenues are coming from the sales of products and services; user subscriptions provided for website users; and other services rendered to the customers.

ADVANTAGES OF E-BUSINESS

The scope for e-business is unlimited. Service providers and business owners may create their own websites and start selling their products and services online which not only allows them direct access to a national market but a global market also. Major advantages of E-Business is summarized below:

Advantages of E-Business

Customer is King

In an e-Business, *customer is king.* There is always a direct access to customers in a digital business. Companies can build direct relationships with customers very easily in a transparent and reliable manner.

Enhanced Customer Trust

Since in an e-Business, direct personal interactions are possible between the business owners and the customers, it creates the impression that the business is trustworthy. Personalized interactions also build customer loyalty in the long term.

Speed and Dynamics

Speed of Service; Ease of Use and Transparency in Transactions are some of the major advantages of E-business.

Location Advantages

Geographic location is no longer a barrier for global collaborations; Global reach to a wider audience enables international E-Marketing

Foolproof Information Management

Foolproof information management the key to a successful e-business. Customer information is easy to gather, store and retrieve online at no or less cost. However, success of an e-business lies in its capability to translate this data into marketable knowledge. Therefore, data management and knowledge/information management deserve more attention in a digital business environment.

Intellectual Capital and Entrepreneurship

Intellectual capital and entrepreneurship are the most important core assets of an E-Business.

Access to Global Markets

E-business provides a virtual global platform for marketing a firm's products and services.

Low Cost Inventory and Better Inventory Management

E–business maximizes supply chain efficiency by ensuring JIT (Just In Time) delivery of products/services at right prices at right places. This, in turn, reduces inventory costs and enables better inventory management practices.

Cost Effective Advertising and Marketing

It is cost-effective for an e-business to advertise online than adopting traditional advertising media. Using digital marketing tools also ensures a global scale marketing campaigns.

E-BUSINESS STRATEGIES

Major business strategies that will help an E-Business develop economically viable business models are, price strategy; purchase strategy; service strategy; business process strategy and ICT strategy.

Price Strategy

Key Factors that drive an E-Business are, unique product features; lower prices; readily available knowledge or information about products and/or services; pricing information; price comparison features; and access to a Discussion Community. Readily available information on prices creates a dynamic pricing market online and therefore the products and/or services offered online are sometimes sold for something other than list prices. The pricing strategy of an e-business should always be based on the theme of cost-savings. Two pricing strategies that may be adopted by an E-business are, Skimming Pricing Strategy and Penetration Pricing Strategy.

Skimming Pricing Strategy

Skimming pricing strategy allows a strategist to set high initial prices for the products and services. This strategy may be adopted if you are the only market leader in your area of business and your products and/or services are unique and there is a niche market for them.

Penetration Pricing Strategy

Penetration pricing strategy allows a strategist to decrease the actual prices of the products and services so that the company can capture a huge market share upon the launch of its e-business. This strategy may be adopted if you operate in a competitive E-Business marketplace.

Purchase Strategy

Purchase strategy of an e-business should focus on the motives behind online purchases. A strategist must ask the following questions before finalizing the purchase strategy for his/her e-business.

- What is the motivation of online customers?
- Is it because of the internet's ability to manage time efficiently by reducing transaction costs?
- Or is it because of positive customer feedbacks posted online?
- Do price advantages play a role in bringing in more potential customers?

Finding answers to such queries is critical for developing a successful purchase strategy for your e-business. Understanding customer behaviour is the key to a successful future strategy.

Service Strategy

In an e-business environment, customer is definitely the king; that is the reason why a lot of significance is attached to customer services in an e-business. An e-business should be able to meet its customer requirements at any given point of time. In order to achieve this, software applications such as CRM (Customer Relationship Management) systems may be integrated with the e-business work environment.

Business Process Strategy

E-business processes should be based on automated business transactions and workflows. This automation may be achieved by the proper integration of all essential software applications in an e-business environment. Since SCM (Supply Chain Management) is a strategic tool for a company's competitiveness, implementation of SCM systems help the company outperform its competitors in a number of ways. The foundation of E-SCM is electronic data interchange (EDI) systems. A successful e-business process strategy focuses on data management; information management; and analysis of business performance analysis, customer behaviour; market trends, and price trends.

Information and Communication Technology Strategy

Information and Communication Technology (ICT) helps an e-business enhance customer relationships; improve its product and/or service features and accelerate decision-making process. As far as customers are concerned, ICT improves customer satisfaction by empowering customers with the availability of quality information. Company may also provide customized or personalized services upon customer request. When it comes to the products and/or services, the company can improve them based on genuine customer feedbacks. An illustration of a number of strategic approaches that should be adopted for the creation of a successful e-business is given below:

Strategic Approaches for an E-Business

Building a Brand

Major advantages of building a brand is that a brand name reflects a company's target business segment which in turn, builds trust in buyers of company's products and services. However on the down side, adequate capital is required to ensure the credibility of the brand among various target segments.

Building Strong Customer Base through Transparency

Building strong customer relationships through transparent dealings will result in more number of satisfied customer. However doing so may result in possible loss of company's power up to certain extent and also there is some risk of being building competitors at company's cost.

Focus on Portal Development

As a result of focusing on web portal development, the portal will gradually become more customer-friendly. Sometimes, greater focus on portal development may delay profitability of the business.

Building Niche Markets

An e-Business may specialize in specific customer service areas and thus build niche markets for its services and products. However, focusing on niche markets may prove to be more demanding. It also requires more capital and resources.

CONSTRAINTS IN E-BUSINESS

Smooth transition of a traditional business to an e-business is possible only if you are able to overcome major constraints such as inadequate infrastructural facilities; traditional mindset of employees and customers; and lack of proper code of conduct over the internet. A summary of major constraints and appropriate measures to be adopted to overcome these constraints are given below:

Inadequate Infrastructural Facilities

Basic infrastructure that is necessary for creating and operating an e-business are high speed internet, quality networking; computers with fast processing units and other hardware equipments.

Resistance to Changing Business Practices

Traditional mindset of the employees and customers may be another constraint that comes in the way of creation of an e-business. Providing training on computer applications and conducting E-commerce awareness programs are two of the best practices that may be adopted to create a team of net savvy workforce.

Lack of Policies and Regulations

Cyberspace still lacks a definite code of conduct and therefore internet users are still worrying about data security and confidentiality of their transactions through internet despite the surety e-commerce sites offer.

Cyber laws are not yet popular and hence users wonder whether there is an appropriate mechanism for settlement of disputes arising out of internet transactions. Another major areas of concern are protection of IPR (intellectual property rights) and lack of mutual confidence and trust among the parties dealing through the Internet.

Slow Responsiveness and Slow Speed of Business

Reluctance from the part of farmers, producers, suppliers and other trade partners to adopt computer and internet technology is a major constraint that hinders the expansion of e-businesses. Some of the major reasons behind this slowness to adopt technology may the place, where the users face severe internet connectivity issues; age where middle aged and elderly people think that IT is beyond their reach; and personality traits where people think that it is waste of time spending time online.

Higher Internet Charges and Low Percent of Internet Penetration

Internet access is more expensive in developing nations where agriculture is the backbone of the economy than that of developed world that focuses on industrialization. Internet penetration is also low in agrarian countries as compared to that of developed nations.

Miscellaneous

Place, business structure and customer demographics may also become constraining factors in the creation and success of an e-business.

CONCLUSION

Internet market is growing at a fast pace all over the world owing to the fact that the future of human civilization is very much dependent on the adoption of advanced technologies in all areas of life and business. And there is no dearth of technological innovations either. Tech-savvy generation has definitely the advantages of *'first movers'* and they seem to know almost 'everything' as knowledge is now available for them 'at their fingertips' and *'information is just a click away'*. The rate of adoption of high end technologies has been very high in all other industrial sectors as compared to agricultural and business sectors. Hence the need of the hour is to address this technological gap exists in business sector so that more and more tech-savvy entrepreneurs may come forward and start contributing to the economic development of the nation.

ABOUT THE AUTHOR

Roby Jose Ciju is the author of *'The Art of Perfect Living'*, an inspirational book based on scriptural wisdom. She is a professional horticulturist and an agribusiness consultant with a Masters Degree in Horticulture and a Post Graduate Diploma in Agri-Supply Chain Management. She has founded www.agrihortico.com, a website dedicated for publishing information on Food & Agriculture Topics. She has written more than 40 books on various topics till date and her best-selling books are, Mushroom Farming, Moringa, Curryleaf, and Growing Ginger, Turmeric and Arrowroot. She may be contacted at roby@agrihortico.com. You may follow agrihortico at https://twitter.com/agrihortico1. Her personal website is available at www.robyjoseciju.com.

Roby Jose Ciju

www.ingramcontent.com/pod-product-compliance
Lightning Source LLC
Chambersburg PA
CBHW020714180526
45163CB00008B/3084